Other Collections in the Series By Sandra de Helen

From Launch Point Press

Poetry for the New Millennium

Poetry for the People: Heavy Verse (2020)

Lesbian Humor is Not an Oxymoron: Light Verse (2019)

Desire Returns for a Visit: Intimate Poems about Lesbian Love (2018)

Praise for the Poetry of Sandra de Helen

Poetry for the People

"Sandra's poetry covers a broad range of experiences and subject matter ... I found her empathy for others, particularly people who've lived with oppression and/or suppression, to be potent and expressed often throughout the work."
~Peter Lautz, poet and author of "Wild Taste"

"Sandra de Helen's title *Poetry for the People* rings true. Her poems, dedicated to kids in cages detained by US immigration, give voice to everyday people and shine light on issues of social justice. I am drawn to this slim collection for its ability to inspire wisdom and hope through pain."
~Cherie Gough, at Amazon

"I loved this book of poetry by Sandra de Helen aptly called *Poetry for the People* as these poems are, indeed, for the people. While the poems are deeply personal, I find them deeply and easily felt and experienced. I got caught up these poems from the dedication which is set amid a graphic of a chain link fence made to keep children in cages – 'May you hold onto the truth that you are loved, you are worthy, you are enough. May you live to be free and to fight for the freedom of all people. #NoKidsinCages.'"
~Sarah June, at Goodreads

Lesbian Humor is Not an Oxymoron

"If you like light-hearted poems with serious undertones, you'll enjoy Sandra's newest offering, a slice of wisdom sprinkled with blood orange humor."
~**Jazzy Mitchell, author of *Undertow* and *You Matter***

"Irreverent while still relevant. Poignant, pungent, playfully pugnacious and peppered with poultry. Sandra de Helen's light verse (which includes letters to Santa and Martians) illuminates the silliest corners of her skylarking sapphist psyche."
~**G.L. Morrison, poet, word lover, and short fiction writer**

"The author isn't kidding that Lesbian Humor is Not an Oxymoron. This book is full of zingers: 'I leaned in for a kiss. She offered me a peppermint.' 'My friend John, a holdover from the union of older men who trained hard to be curmudgeons ...' 'I gave the damned boots away. They were kicking my ass.' 'But you know that world famous Golden Gate? It's orange.' (Just to name a few.) 5.0 out of 5 stars."
~**Kate Kasten, Award-winning author of plays, essays, short stories, and books**

Desire Returns for a Visit

"[Sandra de Helen's] book of poems is a great way to read a truthful, witty, poignant memoir about lesbian love."
~**Judy Grahn, Ph.D., poet, writer, trailblazer**

"It's not often I find poems that speak so directly of and to my lesbian heart. Love poems all, even when love kicks and confuses, this poet portrays the lesbian core."
~**Lee Lynch, novelist, essayist, story writer, trailblazer**

RAINBOW AWARDS HONORABLE MENTION
"The author wrote with lyrical, beautiful sentences that painted pictures in my mind. Her choices in style and presentation were fabulous."
~Elisa Rolle, Rainbow Awards Judge

"From the opening poem to the last 'Dead Reckoning' I found this collection of poetry to be very accessible. In this hectic world where my to do list is a page long, and like Sisyphus never ending, I found myself reading one poem then going on to read several more, doing this over the course of a couple weeks... Many of the titles open with a poem by Emily Dickinson and follow with a response from de Helen's own work. This is a lovely gift."
~E. B. Mulligan, Vine Voice

"This book covers the breadth and depth of a relationship from its exciting beginning to its ending."
~Jazzy Mitchell, author of *Undertow* and many other novels

"These are fresh poems in every sense of the word. Flirty, audacious, original. A fresh take on Dickinson's love of women and words. A brazen exploration of the life cycle of love affairs. This book is an open-mouthed kiss to the reader. It will leave you breathless."
~G.L. Morrison, poet, lover of words, and short fiction writer

Poetry for the New Millennium ~ Volume IV

THE WORLD'S A STAGE

Life in Five Acts

by

Sandra de Helen

2021

A Launch Point Press Trade Paperback Original
THE WORLD'S A STAGE: LIFE IN FIVE ACTS is a work of poetic fiction. Names, characters, places, and incidents are either the product of the author's imagination or are used fictitiously. Any resemblance to actual persons living or dead, business establishments, events, or locales is entirely coincidental.

Copyright © 2021 by Sandra de Helen

All rights reserved. Launch Point Press supports copyright which enables creativity, free speech, and fairness. Thank you for buying the authorized version of this book and for following copyright laws by not using or reproducing any part of this book in any manner whatsoever, including Internet usage, without written permission from Launch Point Press, except in the form of brief quotations embodied in critical reviews and articles. Your cooperation and respect supports authors and allows Launch Point Press to continue to publish the books you want to read.

ISBN: 978-1-63304-230-8
Ebook: 978-1-63304-234-6

FIRST EDITION: First Printing, 2021

Editing: Lori L. Lake
Copyediting: Claudia Kuzmanich
Formatting: Patty Schramm
Book and Cover Design: Lorelei
Cover Image: "May Picture," 1925, oil painting
By Paul Klee [1879-1940], and in the public domain

Portland, Oregon
www.LaunchPointPress.com

*To my sister,
Alberta McCorkle Mobley,
who has known me longer
than anyone still living*

AUTHOR'S FOREWORD

At this stage of my life, it is time to grow sage. Not the plant, but sage as in wise. Whether my words are wise or not is up to the reader to judge, I merely report my experiences and observations. I was raised poor, but was enriched by having parents who read and allowed me to read freely. Books made me want to see, taste, feel, smell, hear, and experience the world. I've taken advantage of every opportunity to do so. Traveling is limited now, but reading is not. Books continue to take me away. I hope this one allows you to do a bit of traveling yourself, back in time maybe, or to be inspired to look at your own life experiences in a new way.

Sandra de Helen
Portland, Oregon
November, 2021

CONTENTS

DEDICATION
AUTHOR'S FOREWORD

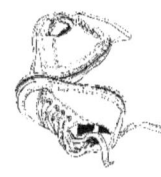

ACT ONE: Childhood

1	Boiled Wool Booties
2	Poor Doctor Cottingham
3	Stemming
4	Dance Class at Three Years Old
6	Dreams of the World
7	Trimming the Tree
9	Tangerine
10	First Day of School
11	Chicanery for My Sister
12	My Favorite Outfit at Six Years Old
13	Blackberry Picking
15	Swimming Lessons
16	Deep Turquoise Blue
17	Aftermath of Death
18	Moving Day
19	Tree as Church
20	Grade School Graduation

ACT TWO: Teenage Years

23	An Education in One Visit
25	Cadillac Confessional
28	Charging for Porn
30	It Didn't Feel Dangerous
31	Molasses is the Color I Remember

33	Dim Love
34	About a Bruise
36	We Took the Wrong Train
37	Shotgun Marriage
38	Dive In
40	Evidence of Love
42	Letter to Myself at Seventeen
43	The Door

ACT THREE: Young Adulthood

47	Faith
48	Prayer
49	The Worst is Over
50	Goddess Moon
52	Peace
53	Gossip
54	Words are Weapons
56	Mendacity
57	Your Soul
58	I Am a Mountain
59	A Way with Words
60	We Make it So

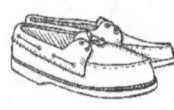

ACT FOUR: Middle Life

65	Erubescent: adjective/*rare* Reddening; blushing.
66	Those Thoughts
67	O Morning Mourning
68	Middle Way
69	Learning to Meditate
70	That's All I Have to Say
61	Not a Homebody
72	Wabi-Sabi Heart

73	Book Signing
74	A Prayer
73	Writing Retreat
76	What Lies Within
77	Goal
78	Mine
79	Moved by the Train
80	Blessings
81	Our Library
83	A Little Austere
84	Why Did You Invite Her?
85	Self-Made
86	Gratitude

ACT FIVE: Later Life

91	Artifacts
92	Broke Broker Broken
93	Still Here, Rain
94	Scottish Ancestors
95	Enough is Enough
96	The Morning
97	Afterwards, Day
98	Sight
99	Putting On
100	Fun With Aging
102	Raves Are for the Young
100	Where There's Smoke
103	All That Remains
104	Sunrise

AFTERWORD
ACKNOWLEDGMENTS
ABOUT THE POET

All the world's a stage,
And all the men and women merely players;
They have their exits and their entrances;
And one man in his time plays many parts . . .

As You Like It
by William Shakespeare
Act II, Scene 7

Act One: Childhood

'Tis much when sceptres are in children's hands . . .

Henry VI
Act IV, Scene 1

Boiled Wool Booties

Items remain from my first day home:
white lawn dress with pintucked bib,
tiny ribbons. One sock.

Palest green boiled wool booties.
Shoes almost.
As small as my little finger now.

My first photo shows my fat little feet
wearing these booties. I can almost feel them
keeping me warm that January day.

I rode home next to Mom and Dad
in our Model A Ford, wrapped in flannel
and wool, inhaling cold Missouri air

and my parents' laughter as they
brought me home. I was the first live one,
after three dead babies.

Poor Doctor Cottingham

Mom laughs as she tells me
again how she left me lying
in my crib, a few months old

as she ran down to Aunt Annie's
house, using the nearest telephone
to call good Doctor Cottingham.

Her constipated baby who never
goes without having an enema.
This time no water came out

after mama gave baby the whole
bag, so she gave baby another
whole bag and still nothing came out.

Baby was crying and crying.
Please, Dr. Cottingham, what's
a mother to do?

Can you imagine? Mom asks,
poor Dr. Cottingham, I was
always bothering him with something.

This time I ask what he suggested.
Oh, I don't recall, I expect he told me
you'd go eventually, and you did.

Stemming

It isn't difficult really,
stemming wild huckleberries.
Not when you're three years old

your fingers are dexterous
and it is your nature to please.
Me and mama on the big front porch

out in the country, the evenings too hot
to sit in the house anyway.
Mama sews on buttons,

mends shirts: things more suited
for mother-size hands. Me with my apron
over sun-browned legs, bare feet
sticking straight out,

speckled enamel bowl full of berries
between my knees. I stem until dark so we
can make pies for when Dad comes home
from painting houses in Arkansas.

Dance Class at Three Years Old

The kids were performing cartwheels,
turning somersaults frontwards
and back, throwing themselves

in circles across the room
head over heels without hands
touching the floor,

or even—best of all—walking about
on their hands, their feet straight up
above them. Some were tap-dancing

some were turning in circles
with their arms in circles
over their heads, it was mad chaos

with everyone smiling from ear to ear
unless they were shouting to each other
Hey Judy Hey Sharon Hey Joey Hey Hey

Until Miss Zoey clapped her hands
one two three and it was dead silent.
She brought out a long cord

with a microphone attached,
turned it on and went round the room. We
have new pupils here today children,

so let's all say our names, here we go.
And they did: Nancy, Janet, Mike,
David, Johnny, as
Mom stood holding my hand.

I shrank into the wall, trying to
escape, trying to get out the door,
ending up at the crack of the door
with nowhere to go.

Still, I could not get my name
over the lump in my throat.

A few weeks later I was standing on the table,
singing into the mic.

Dreams of the World

I am nothing.
I will never be anything.
I cannot wish to be anything.
Bar that, I have in me all the dreams of the world.
~Álvaro de Campos, "The Tobacco Shop"

In a four-room house on Route 66
overlooking Dead Man's Curve, a four-year-old
girl learns to read from a book from the dump

while sitting on her Dad's knee. Every night
her head is filled with dreams of a wider world—
visions of places called England and Ireland and
France

where people live across the sea. There are houses
with bathtubs and running water. Palaces with queens.

There are buildings filled with books.
She will visit them all one day.

Trimming the Tree

Dad and I went to the woods on our own property
to cut a Christmas tree. It snowed the night before,
and I was bundled in thick leggings over my dress,

coat buttoned up to my neck, mittens, galoshes,
and stocking cap. Mom always
dressed me properly before Dad died.

We tromped around in the damp glistening snow
looking for a cedar of just-right size.
When we found one alone in a clearing,

Dad chopped it down in a flash. He dragged it back
to the house as I ran ahead and back, filled with
delight.

At home, Dad sawed the bottom of the trunk flat,
and hammered in boards to make it stand.
He shook the snow from the branches,
and brought the tree to the front door

where Mom waited. She brushed off the snow
and took our boots to keep the floral linoleum clean.

The tree stood in front of the window
facing the highway.
Mom and Dad worked together to string the lights,
which would stay lit all night on Christmas Eve.

They placed the few ornaments we owned, including a shiny tin star encapsulating one white bulb. At last it was time for real lead tinsel and I was allowed to help.

When we stood back to admire our handiwork, that tinsel shone like ice. In memories of my childhood home, the entire night glitters.

Tangerine

The peel comes away in my hands,
no effort, no need for tools.
The aroma bursts forth
before the skin is pierced.

The tiny sections give up their skin
at the slightest pressure of my teeth,
the juice runs sweetness across my tongue
and down my yearning throat.

Once these were available only at Christmas,
their scent as evocative as the cedar tree
standing in front of the window,
showing off its jewelry to the neighbors.

Memories of a Christmas pageant,
being draped in white robes,
crowned with a halo, reciting
the Bible version of the birth
one month after the death of my father.

Santa came after, bearing small brown
paper bags with nuts, a few candies
and that deep orange tangerine.

This small globe of sunshine
sits in my hand, holding
then revealing, long ago memories.

First Day of School

This is the cloak room, where we hang up
our coats and leave our lunch boxes. Also
store our galoshes or rubbers, in case of rain.

This is the girls' bathroom. Come along.
In the big room, you will sit in this row.
The rows are arranged by grade level,
these two are first grade, then second, third,
fourth and so on up through eighth.

When it's time for school, I'll ring the bell,
and we all gather to march over to the church
for morning prayers. I'll ring the bell again

after recesses and lunch. You always return
to your seat when you hear the bell. You
understand? No talking during school.

You understand that? Do you have friends here? No?
I see. Well you're going to sit here between Naomi
in front of you, and Bobby in back. You can talk to them
at recess. Not now.

Stand by your desk, we're about to go
to morning prayers. Is there anything you
would like to ask me?

Yes. What's a cloak?

Chicanery for My Sister

When you were old enough to sit
in a highchair and not yet weaned

from her breast, you already knew
you were never going to eat like a normal person.

Just like her. She thought I could coax you to eat.
I helped you to sleep by shaking your crib.

Every day. Every night. Shake, shake, shake.
While you ah-ah-ah-ed.

Now you sit, not eating. Big light blue eyes
beams of non-compliance daring me

to dream up some chicanery to tempt
you to eat. Airplanes don't interest you.

Watching me chew is for the birds.
Tap-dancing? That makes you laugh.

Mom slips in the spoon. Again. And again.
I spend your toddlerhood dancing for your guffaws.

My Favorite Outfit at Six Years Old

Double layers of whitest voile
kept bright with bluing or
bleach or sun or all three,

soft from years of being laundered
by hand in Missouri rain water.

Now Mom's hands pull the voile
from living room windows
and create my favorite blouse.

Wide deep ruffle makes an off-shoulder neckline
with elastic to hold it securely in any position.
It fits me perfectly and stays inside my waistband

as I twirl and twirl showing off
my ballerina legs and new circle skirt
made from bark cloth slipcovers.

Blackberry Picking

Babysit or pick? Choose one.
I loved picking blackberries,
stuffing my mouth as the sweet juice ran down my chin,
and I tried to hide my sin from Grandma.

We started right after daybreak. Dew clung
to the leaves, the thorns, the deep purple gems
themselves. We each had our buckets to fill.

Mine was a gallon pail, the bale wrapped
in cotton fabric scraps, which did nothing
to lessen the tension as the weight strained
my seven-year-old arms.

I could have chosen to stay home with Grandpa
and my baby sister, thereby avoiding the one hundred
and one chiggers that attached themselves

to my body, lining up around the waistband
of my underpants, clustering under my
arms and ankles, hiding between my toes.

But I chose to be with Grandma in the
sun. She mopped her face with one of
Grandpa's hankies. She rolled and smoked

one cigarette after the other, the cancer stick
hanging from the corner of her mouth,
ashes spilling onto her housedress.

After our buckets were filled, we gathered
a few more plump berries, popped them
into our grinning mouths,

and made our way back to the house. Grandma
swabbed me all over with alcohol, burning my scratches
from the briars while killing the chiggers.

I understood it was for my own good.
At supper we ate our gleaning
with sugar and clotted cream.

Swimming Lessons

My mother's voice saved my life the day
the boat turned over. I remembered her giving me
swimming lessons: The water will hold you up.

All you have to do is trust. Just lie back and let the water
hold you up. Breathe. Simply breathe. Relax, keep
your toes up,

concentrate on keeping the tips of your toes
out of the water. That's it. Any time you're tired
of swimming, or you feel yourself growing

weak, turn over, let the water do the work.
Shut your eyes. Listen to the world under the water.
Feel the air on your toes. Listen for the fish. Hear them?

A school of minnows swam by on their way to the shade
under the pier. You'll be there yourself soon.
When your bottom touches the ground,
stand up and walk out.

Deep Turquoise Blue

Deep turquoise blue on a billboard
stirred a three-year-old heart
and made her want to eat the color.

She chewed the back of the front
seat of the Model A Ford instead,
where her Dad drove, and Mom stared ahead.

Biting and shutting her eyes,
feeling the waves flood her chest
with exquisite blue shivers.

Her hands clenched the seat
as her sturdy legs rode
the floor of the old car.

She wanted to talk about
her feelings, the beauty,
the warmth it gave.

Instead, she took the color
to bed that night, and rode
it like a wave, feeling the lift
of deep turquoise blue.

Aftermath of Death

Moths in the light fixture tell me
how long it has been since she went to work
and I stayed home to shake the baby to sleep.

She used to dust the bed springs, iron sheets,
wash windows on Mondays after the laundry
was rubbed by hand and hung outside with pins.

Now she makes shoes by day, waits tables by night.
I go to school, then my baby sister and I play
house. I'm the mama. There is no Dad any more.

Moving Day

I write the date in pencil. White porch ceiling
a perfect canvas: May 11,1955. For the first time
in my eleven years I am a town girl.
It's a dazzling day and I'm expected
only to keep six-year-old sister out of trouble.

Woo hoo! I race around the yard and behind
our brick house, clamber and scramble up the steep hill
to woods unlike our previous acres
and find mossy patches
to loll and roll on. A creek.

Huge trees, some tumbled down,
just right for climbing up to yet other trees
into whose arms I can recline.

I've forgotten about my sister who has gone off
on her own adventure and found a friend living
next door through a grove on another side.

We meet when I find the neighbor's house
from the back and we agree to keep
our newfound freedom secret.

Tree as Church

Every Saturday morning as the sun climbs
over the hills and brushes the top of the
sycamore at the side of our red brick house,

I don my summer attire, grab my latest
tome, slip out the front door, down the stairs and
I climb—to the platform twenty feet up the
tree: my sanctuary.

Step-dad built it for only me. This is where I pray
for deliverance from the misery of childhood
with a mother who drinks and hits, never cooks or eats,

doesn't care what time I come home
unless she needs me to babysit. Saturdays,
I can count on several hours
before the parents are up.

My sister will come out and call me
to make breakfast when she awakes. Until then
The Well of Loneliness prepares me for a future
as an outsider, in a way different from the one I know.

Grade School Graduation

Vintage gown, altered to fit me
not the era. Powder blue moiré silk,
sweetheart neckline, fitted waist
and gently gathered skirt that falls to the floor.

I feel like a princess with my long blond hair,
uncut since second grade, never permed.

My classmates wear knee-length
strapless dresses in pastels with rows of ruffles,
two or three crinolines underneath.

Their hairdos, every single one of them: up,
with a bundle of curls at the nape.

As I walk down the aisle, Salutatorian side by side
with the Valedictorian I hold my head high in pride:
second best in a second-hand dress.

Act Two:
Teenage Years

Woe to the land that's governed by a child...

Richard III
Act II, Scene 3

An Education in One Visit

Janet and I walked four miles in the noonday sun
with our bottles of unopened Pepsi
on our way to the lookout Tower

which was seven miles from town. It was July
in Missouri, 1956. We had eaten our melting
    chocolate bars
and were desperate for something to drink,

but hadn't brought a bottle opener.
We crossed the spongy asphalt road
to the stone mansion to ask the owner

for help. She said come on in girls
I was just giving myself a pedicure.
We searched each other's faces for a clue

but found none. She brought out tumblers
of ice and poured our own Pepsis for us
while we each used the powder room.

As we finished our drinks and headed back out
into the heat, she asked did one of you girls
light a match in the bathroom?

What? No. Pedicures? Matches?
We were mystified and couldn't wait

to escape this lunatic's clutches.

She offered to drive us into town,
but we ran away claiming we needed
the exercise.

I nearly fell into the small stone pool
on my way out. The fish there were as big
as the ones my grandma had in her cow pond,

and just as silent. But they weren't catfish.
This woman had created a pond
exclusively for her goldfish.

Who was she? Pedicures, lit matches
and outdoor goldfish. I wanted to be her
when I grew up.

Cadillac Confessional

Forgive me for being twelve,
blond, a good kid, a bad
reporter. The front seat
refuses to keep

its quiet, the rest stops refuse
any longer to withhold
their brutality secrets from
our faces. I've fallen for
the fifty-year-

old American Shriner who
gives rides.
I've invoked the goddess.

I've desecrated – no – I
flamencoed cemeteries and
that led to fiery tap-dancing
With sisters, with
Tiny nymphs.

        A breast
touching arm, the tongue
hooked inside teeth.
I'll get over it and
bring myself about all over

again: the predatory American
the groping banker
with the hands. But I'll not
cry tears dripping
someone else's salt. At twelve
I was prematurely aged
by a middle-aged Shriner

                in the oversized
celadon Cadillac past Rolla.
                My mother
shamed me into accepting
the fiver. I could die.

That Shriner is now a
hundred-year-old corpse in a grave
in the shape of my slipper.

My foot is a beautiful appendage.
I dance on graves. I don't
indulge in abandonment.

I dance flamencos on the grave
of the patriarchy.
I eviscerate the guts from
the story and let those
intestines sing their

tales again
and again. I harmonize.
I'm a good reporter
who can't help accepting
life, grasping toward
the future. This is not
the finale.

All of my finales
are prologues.

Charging for Porn

I found the photographs
in the linen closet.
Eight-by-ten black-and-
white glossies. Like
head shots. Except you
couldn't actually see
their faces.

They were pictures of a
man and a woman
having sex. In one
picture, my favorite,
they were intertwined
so you could see
both their genitals.

His penis was long
enough to be both
inside her vagina
and outside, too
so a person could
see what it looked
like, veins and all.

I was twelve. I
stared and puzzled

and turned the
pictures every
which way, even
over, hoping for
names on the backside.

Was this my mom? Which
boyfriend could it be?
I couldn't keep this
delicious secret to
myself.

I began to bring my girlfriends
to the house to see the pictures.
Should I charge for porn?
I knew my boy friends
sometimes charged their
pals to look at their
twenty-five-cent
eight-page bibles.

No, I shared my prize
for the cost of silence.

It Didn't Feel Dangerous

when she told me to lie next to her
in her bed in the basement, to wrap my arms
around her body and tilt my head just so.

we were only practicing.

> it didn't occur to me she would
> ever hurt me, or could. what we
> were doing felt good,
> after all.
>
> and we were just practicing.

she taught me how to kiss,
and how to move my hips and
keep my long hair out of the way.

> Then one night after watching Elvis on TV,
> the boys were walking us home
> when she suddenly disappeared and
> left me alone with Ronnie.

There were no soft kisses, no
wrapping of arms, or tilting my head.
I said no. To no avail.
I gasped. I cried.

And I walked home alone, bleeding.

Molasses is the Color I Remember . . .

. . . when I think of the night you
kissed me for the first time. We sat
on my Mom's green couch in the
living room that was painted
chartreuse with forest green ceiling.

The hardwood floors gleamed
beneath throw rugs of yellow green,
forest green, or black. The triangular
coffee table held a triangular ashtray
that will outlive us all, no matter that
Mom threw it at every husband and
boyfriend she ever fought with in her
jealous rages.

You and I were new and I was innocent.
I couldn't speak for the lump in my throat
from all the jammed-up words I
wouldn't learn to say out loud for
many years.

In a few weeks you would ask me to marry you
And I would have the good sense to say
no, I had to go to high school first.

But this night, this warm summer
night when I was thirteen and you
were home on leave from the Air Force,
you held my face in your hands, tipped my chin
And gently pressed your lips to mine.

Just before I closed my eyes, I
saw the twinkle in your brown
eyes.

Dim Love

Doubt me, my dim companion!
Why, God would be content
With but a fraction of the love
Poured thee without a stint.
~Emily Dickinson

How could I not doubt your love
when you call me your dim companion?
You say you've given all, when you have gifts

you haven't acknowledged. I have no time
or inclination to give myself to one
who doesn't know her own depths. Before you empty

your bucket of love upon my head,
splash some upon your own
dewy cheeks.

About a Bruise

The first bruise he gave me
should have sent me running
looking in another direction
for a way out of my mother's
house.

It was 1959. Summer in a
tiny town in Missouri. I wanted
out and I couldn't survive another
three years. I had a sort of plan. If
I got pregnant I could go to a
home for unwed mothers. I could
finish high school and give up my
baby for adoption and go to work.
Never go back home.

There was a boy. He wanted me.
Our mothers were friends, so going
out with him was never a problem.
One night at the drive-in movie, I
didn't do something he wanted me
to do. Or respond quickly enough,
or answer in the way he thought I
should, and he had had a lot of beer.
So he grabbed my ear and twisted it.
Hard. For a long time.

The next day the top of my right ear was blue black. And so sore I gasped when I touched it. I wore my hair down, in spite of the mid-summer heat. And I never said a word.

We Took the Wrong Train

I wanted to leave home, in the worst way. So I left in the worst way. Not by growing up and going to college or getting a job, not by catching the four o'clock out of town, not by Greyhound or thumbing a ride.

Your brothers were grown and gone. One to the Navy, one to marriage and a good job in the city. You secretly wore your mother's underwear, and sometimes still wet the bed. You graduated high school as team captain and major alcoholic, but you were lazing around the house, refusing to leave the nest.

That summer I saw you as my way out. I was fifteen, you were eighteen and still chasing me. We fell into bed in the middle of the day, and by the end of the month I knew we were expecting.

We were on a fast train to disaster.

Shotgun Marriage

He put the belt around my life,
—I heard the buckle snap,
And turned away, imperial,
My lifetime folding up . . .
~Emily Dickinson

He didn't know better, he was trapped
as I was, and only three years older.
But he was the man, the husband,

the soon-to-be father, and I
was a caged animal, wild with longing
for freedom. Time tamed neither of us,
but eventually set us free.

Dive In

Our wedding night was spent at Taylor Cottages
Motel in Jefferson City, Missouri the town where
I was born only fifteen years earlier.

I'm guessing Mom and Dad hadn't dreamed
I'd return so soon to make them grandparents,
although my dad died when I was seven.

That night, Ronnie drank a six-pack of cheap
beer that someone bought him. We ate hot dogs
and went to bed before dark. There was no TV,
no sex, and nothing to discuss.

I was three months pregnant and exhausted. All
I could think about was how I dove into this mess
believing that I would somehow be delivered
from my horrible home life.

Now I had jumped from the frying pan into hellfire.
Within three more months I would be told I'd made
my bed and I could come home no more,

before six months were out I'd have a
broken nose, a broken pelvis, and been
hit more times than I could count.

One day I would learn that I had to stay in the marriage six years before I was old enough to divorce.

I survived those six years, and eventually thrived. If I could live my life over, would I again dive in?

Evidence of Love

You said you loved me more than
life itself. You said I meant the
world to you. You said I was the
one and you'd die if I didn't say
I love you back.

You broke my nose, blacked my
eyes, and cut my lip. People noticed
my "car accident" and you promised
you'd never hit me again.

After that you hit my head or my
stomach. Blows designed to never
show. You said I made you hit me, if
only I didn't make you so angry. My
very *being* made you angry.

You tried to kill our baby while he
was still in my womb. You merely
broke my pubic bone. The baby
lived.

I was trapped in this torture until I
was twenty-one. Old enough to get
a lawyer without a parent's consent.
Unlike our forced marriage when our
mothers "consented" to conspire.

You begged me not to leave you. You swore you loved me. Enough to kill our son if I tried to take him with me.

The evidence of your love lives on in our son.

Letter to Myself at Seventeen

You're already a wife and mother,
you work full time to help support
your family. You're taking night classes
to get a high school diploma you'll never see,

and you wonder whether you'll escape
this entrapment with a battering husband,
as miserable as you are in a life
you didn't bargain for.

What can I tell you? I swear it will get better.
But time is involved. A lot of time.
Change your reading habits, start with Plato,
and a paperback dictionary.

Read on the bus on your way to work,
stop worrying about your looks,
instead, focus on your brain.

You're not fat, you're not ugly,
and you are far from stupid.
Do not listen to your husband,
listen to the small voice in your head

telling you life will get better.
Fill your head with lofty goals,
let your imagination soar
where you can't. Yet.

The Door

I opened the door and the wind came in
bringing every dirty trick you thought of
along with it—gathering under the table

ganging up in the corners, trying
to look like innocent dust bunnies
swirling around my ankles

pulling me flat on the hardwood floor
dragging the rug out from under me when
I was carrying our son in my nine-month belly

or holding a hot peach pie the first Thanksgiving
with your mom and brother, aunt and granddad
all looking on, watching the peaches slide down the wall

six years the door stood open while the tricks stacked up
and tumbled over tripping me every time I hurried
to soothe your troubled daydreams landing me
in another nightmare

until one night the police held you back as I packed a bag
and shut that door behind me.

Act Three: Young Adulthood

Doubt thou the stars are fire; Doubt that the sun doth move; Doubt truth to be a liar; But never doubt I love.

Hamlet
Act II, Scene 2

Faith

Faith is a fine invention
For gentlemen who see;
But microscopes are prudent
In an emergency!
~Emily Dickinson

Born and raised in the First Christian Church,
sporting a perfect attendance pin
that reflected eight years of showing up on Sundays,

we left that church after my first step-father died.
But not before he and I were baptized
on the same day.

At eleven, I began a years-long exploration
of faith and spirituality. Now I place my faith
in Science.

Prayer

Prayer is the little implement
Through which men reach
Where presence is denied them.
They fling their speech
By means of it in God's ear;
~Emily Dickinson

When friends ask for prayers I light a candle,
and think of them, feeling love, sympathy,
fear, sorrow, as they traverse a difficult journey.

Praying to a god in which I don't believe would be hollow
would not honor my friends' requests. Yet, there is
no need for me to fling words of disrespect.

My friends seek assistance. I do what I am able.

The Worst is Over

*. . . When Fate hath taunted last
And thrown her furthest stone,
The maimed may pause and breathe,
And glance securely round . . .*
~Emily Dickinson

When you've hit rock bottom,
when the poorest possible outcome
has come, when you can no longer
drop, but must begin the climb
back up, the worst is over.

From the depths of the well of loneliness,
look up. Above is the sky. It may be gray,
or blue; it may have clouds, or wind, or both.
Perhaps the night is crowded with moon and stars.
One thing sure: the sky is enormous
and your life holds infinite possibility.

Breathe it in.

Goddess Moon

The moon is distant from the sea,
And yet with amber hands
She leads him, docile as a boy,
Along appointed sands.
He never misses a degree;
Obedient to her eye,
He comes just so far toward the town,
Just so far goes away.
~Emily Dickinson

I love the moon as much as anyone, have worshipped
her full round face since I was in third grade.
One—only one—night my friend Mary Lou
was allowed to stay over.

We went out and sat on the swing set in the light
of the full moon. We vowed to always remember
each other every full moon for the rest of our lives.

The goddess moon featured large throughout my entire
childhood and adolescence. But especially
during the early days of feminism.
I attended rituals that made me giggle

when I was supposed to be solemn. I wore garments
I could easily discard in order to dance naked in the
moonlight.

In midlife I moved to Oregon where seeing a full moon
is a rare occurrence, as the night sky is so often overcast.
I stopped dancing in the moonlight, and walked
in the rain instead.

Through it all, I keep my promise to Mary Lou.
I haven't seen her for more than half a century,
but I remember her when the moon is full.
Such is the power of the goddess.

Peace

I many times thought peace had come,
When peace was far away;
~Emily Dickinson

Peace floats there, near the horizon
—just out of reach—as I swim
the seas of life. Love is all around me,
holding me, warming me, saving me

in order that I may continue to strive
for the quieting of the mind,
the calm to allow me to accept myself.

Gossip

The leaves, like women, interchange
Sagacious confidence;
Somewhat of nods, and somewhat of
Portentous inference,
The parties in both cases
Enjoining secrecy,—
Inviolable compact
To notoriety.
~Emily Dickinson

Gossip is never an inviolable compact,
however often we tell ourselves
we can keep a secret. Words shared

between two people—male or female—
will be repeated to another sooner
rather than later. We may wish to protect

from notoriety, the shame of everyone knowing
the secret, but we are not plant life interchanging
our tasty secrets.

We are only human.

Words are Weapons

Words. Stick and stones that break my
bones cannot compare to the wounding
of words: who do you think you are?
It's good enough, stop complaining.
I'll give you something to cry about.

Four's a whore. I can't trust you. Who
are you looking at now? You want
him? You f***ing him? I'll kill you
and our child both before I'll let you
leave me.

I only hire divorced women. I know they
need the job. I can't give you a raise,
you don't have a wife and family to
support. Even though you had the
highest score, we can't send you to
computer school for three weeks, we're
sending Emery instead. What would
people think if we sent you and Dave
on the same trip?

I'm not going to move you into that
position because you tend to brag on
your work. I feel more comfortable with
Paul for some reason.

I know you're a lesbian, but do you have to talk about it all the time? I don't like to hear about it. It's fine with me whatever you want, just don't talk about it. Especially in front of . . .

(To my daughter:) I'm so happy for your mom that she is okay with going to hell for being a lesbian. I'm glad she's made her peace with it.

These words are the things that wound and scar. Love is the only balm.

Mendacity

In order to say the word
mendacious aloud, one must
hail from the deep South. You
must know its meaning from
inside your dark soul to your
twinkling devil eyes.

When you say the word
mendacious aloud, even those
who know its meaning will be
charmed by your use of it.
They will believe you mean
them no harm, no harm a'tall.

I know your mendacity. It is
stitched across the plains of
my heart as if I'd been struck
down by lightning and had
to be brought back to life by
electric shock.

I begged you not to lie to
me. I suffered your excesses
as if they were my own. In
the end you flew away
like a migrating moth disguised
as a butterfly.

Your Soul

Of all the souls that stand create
I have elected—One . . .
~Emily Dickinson

You consume the molecule, you wait
for the mystical, maybe spiritual experience.
Your body comes alive one atom at a time

until every atom is spinning, joining the dance
of the room, mingling with the dust motes,
the streaming sunlight. You feel your blood

rushing to sing with the color of your shirt.
Scarlet makes a buzzing noise and creates a tingle
in your scalp. Turquoise thrums deep

in your belly. Late that night you realize
you have sunk deep into the music
coming from a stereo and know with certainty

this is what death is. Like sleep, but without dreams.
Like wakefulness, but without worry.
Consciousness remains after the body is no longer.
Aware without care. Your soul.

I Am a Mountain

...Which, sir, are you, and which am I,
Upon an August day?
~Emily Dickinson

I am a mountain, named by those
who love me, by those who hate me,
names I never call myself.

I am a mountain unmoved by anything
less than love. My head bears the beginnings
of winter though I cover it in shades of summer.

My feet are covered with flowers, vines, and paths,
though rocky, lead to love and more love.
I am a myriad of daisies, my petals waving in the breezes

caused by life rushing past, so fast I scarcely
catch a glimpse.
I am all things, the same as you. We are all, all.

A Way with Words

He ate and drank the precious words,
His spirit grew robust;
He knew no more that he was poor,
Nor that his frame was dust.
He danced along the dingy days,
And this bequest of wings
Was but a book. What liberty
A loosened spirit brings!
~Emily Dickinson

The ubiquitous, generic "he"
describes me perfectly, except
I was born female.

I came to life when I learned to read.
Books saved me from the life of poverty
I was born into. Gave me liberty,

showed me a world without
my leaving the house. Until I did.
Books illuminated the way.

Read them, write them,
words are the light.

We Make it So

We choose to create this world day by day
we rise from our dreams to show
our façade, to manifest our thoughts,

knowingly or still asleep. Every step
another choice for good or bad, every
choice another branch or twist
or turn in the road.

We daydream ourselves into
existence, or fearfully obsess
our nightmares into reality.
The word is god.

A pie in my mind is sure
to be a pie on my plate
by dinnertime if I
visualize it clearly
with its flaky crust,
juicy cherries topped
with hand-whipped
cream.

A walk in the salt water pool
won't happen unless

I see myself carrying
that gym bag into the athletic club
smiling as I leave with a spring
in my step, proud as I check yes
on my exercise list for the third
time this week.

Act Four: Middle Life

And now let's go hand in hand, not one before another.

The Comedy of Errors
Act V, Scene 1

Erubescent: adjective
rare Reddening; blushing.

There was a time when my third eye was visible.
To my dismay, it would light from within,
a deep vermilion, giving my forehead
a glow that outshone my flaming cheeks,

the rising flush of my throat, and drew attention
from the silence that came instead of prepared speech.
Eventually I would fret words up and over
the squawky lump at the base of my tongue,

gasp my way through the two or three paragraphs,
then sit and dab my now purple brow into submission.

Only one person ever guessed that spot
was not only erubescent, but erogenous.

Those Thoughts

A thought went up my mind today
That I have had before,
But did not finish—some way back,
I could not fix the Year,
Nor where it went—nor why it came . . .
~Emily Dickinson

My mind is a grand canyon with walls springing up
at every turn built of hundreds of layers of every color.

A stream of thought wanders along the bottom,
sometimes warm, crystal clear, sparkling with mineral
    pools,

whirling energy. Sometimes rushing, muddy
after a storm,
filled with debris, opaque with mystery.

Now and then, a stray thought I've seen before
will catch at the edge of a stone, then disappear

so completely I'm not certain I ever saw it.
Sometimes, I capture it and hold it to the light.

O Morning Mourning

O mourning dove, you know my sorrow
you call my name, lancing the wound
of my grief as I wander the garden

seeking relief that refuses to grow
among the lilacs. Further afield
are the bleeding hearts the wild purple pansies

but nothing to soothe my aching soul.
No one brings my love to me, no winged creature
sings or cries a familiar name,

only you, mourning dove, morning
and evening your cooing incessantly
reminding me I am alone.

Middle Way

A Buddhist monk I am not. They divest
themselves of worldly goods, give it
all away. Dressed in a simple uniform,
bearing only one bowl, they depend on
others for their minute meals.

Sleep on the floor. Wake before the sun. Pray
all day for three years. I pledged to be a *bodhisattva*.
Received a Tibetan name. Sat in silence for ten days.

Except when I didn't. Except for the times
I sneaked away to talk and laugh. Made my friend laugh
in the cafeteria.

This is my middle way. I live as simply as I am able.
I follow the right ways of living the best I can.
I honor the lives of all sentient beings.

I have much more to sacrifice in order to honor
my commitment to helping others achieve
the enlightenment I haven't achieved myself.

Learning to Meditate

Beneath the surface of my shiny monkey mind
is a dank and rancid cesspool of self-pity,
revenge fantasies, and grudges so old their wrinkles
have dirt in them. No one wants me
to shine light on those nether regions.

Far below, deeper than the mushy pool
of grievances, there are injuries so ancient
they've been compacted until they are fossils,
diamonds, and thunder eggs containing scenes
from all the lifetimes this soul has experienced.

Forgive me if I slosh a bit of malodorous crap
on my shoe as I do my best to excavate
the glittering truth that will light its own way.

That's All I Have to Say

One impossible thing before I make
breakfast, that's what you ask
of me.

I can't explain my life with its high
hills and deep valleys. Let the river
tell you why it flows.

Let the clouds speak of why they
lower or not, let their shapes tell you
the meaning of existence.

See the desert tortoise grow and change
with only sand and sun
and heat as scenery.

Listen to the crow. She has more words
to speak of life than I do
before breakfast.

Not a Homebody

I was born with a terrible, horrible, pretty bad
case of wanderlust. When I began to crawl,
I didn't stop at the fence, I crawled out

into the gravel road, scraped my tender knees
and kept on going. Worried about the thin skin
of my feet, I didn't walk until I got my first pair

of shoes with leather bottoms when I was
thirteen months. Then I walked to the next farm
where they had goats to play with and other animals

my size. We only had a cow. When I got a bike,
I rode to nearby towns. When I got a car,
I drove to the edges of the continent.

My friend Tamara said if you want things
to be like home, stay home. Traveling
is exciting, educational, mysterious, surprising,

memorable and sometimes uncomfortable.
I won't stop wandering until I lose my lust
for living.

Wabi-Sabi Heart

Sometime in the distant past I made a decision
to wrap it up. My heart that is. Like a Japanese vase,
the many breaks and cracks have been mended over
    the years,

filled with the liquid gold of memory, so even
the most severe damage has a *wabi-sabi*[1]
aspect now, an appearance of *kintsukuroi*.[2]

Still, I wrapped my heart of *kintsugi*[3] and
stored it away, kept it safe.

That thing with feathers, that tiny wren of hope
lives inside. In the dark. In the shadowy closet
of a dream of a relationship that never was

and never will be, but the one to which
I maintain vows.

Unless I unwrap my beautiful *kintsugi* heart
no one will ever see it, no one will ever hold
it in her hand, ever again.

Unless I break those vows, and maybe my heart
(again), no one will ever again experience
my *wabi-sabi* gift.

~~~

1. **Wabi-sabi** literally means *simplicity* and *serenity* and is part of a I world view centered on acceptance of transience and imperfection.
2. **Kintsukuroi** literally means *mended with gold* and emphasizes the beauty and utility of breaks and imperfections
3. **Kintsugi** is the I art of repairing broken pottery, usually filling in, piecing, or jointing

Book Signing

I'm nobody! Who are you?
Are you nobody, too?
Then there's a pair of us—don't tell!
They'd banish us, you know.

How dreary to be somebody!
How public, like a frog
To tell your name the livelong day
To an admiring bog!
~Emily Dickinson

My lifelong dream: to sign my name
in books I authored for devoted readers.
As if the ritual would bestow approval.

May as well kiss a frog as to trust
in fantasy. Nothing can replace a loving mother.

A Prayer

. . . Judgment twinkled, too
That one so honest be extant
As take the tale for true
That "Whatsoever you shall ask,
Itself be given you."
~Emily Dickinson

They say "All prayers are answered,
though sometimes the answer is no."

They say "I helps them who help themselves,"
tossing the prayer back on the one who prays.

Emily Dickinson often invoked I, the heavens,
even cherubim and others, yet she saw
we make our own lives what they are.

I pray for forgiveness. Not to I,
but to the ones I've wronged. The answer
is sometimes yes.

Writing Retreat

Striking an artichoke attitude, I point
my hair slightly to the right and set off
for the train, pushing my suitcase filled

with bold bits of butter, and one bothersome
bright yellow lemon, and I'm off for a week
of sitting the dogs. Cats are far more prevalent in my life,

but a harsh round or two of barking can be bracing
after months of damp train whistling.

I will briskly strip my own leaves, find the way
to my artichoke heart, and with one slippery squeeze,
see if I can manage an authentic tear.

One not caused by that caustic lemon.
Here goes.

What Lies Within

Experiment to me
Is every one I meet.
If it contain a kernel?
The figure of a nut
Presents upon a tree,
Equally plausibly;
But meat within is requisite,
To squirrels and to me.
~Emily Dickinson

When I venture out into the world,
to meet new people, give me the one
who knows how to speak

of current events, deep thoughts,
hard questions of life.

Even the squirrels require
substance in their sustenance.

The squirrels and I have had enough
of empty heads, withered hearts.
Open up and show us what lies within.

Goal

Each life converges to some centre
Expressed or still;
Exists in every human nature
A goal...
~Emily Dickinson

All my life, I have had goals,
taken steps to reach them,
set newer, higher ones. I've been told
I was goal-driven.

Everyone seeks something,
is driven by some thing or place
or feeling they wish to find or achieve.

The bigger question is why?
Why this goal and not the other?
What lies within? What is this
quest I am on? What is the prize?

Mine

Mine by the right of the white election!
Mine by the royal seal!
Mine by the sign in the scarlet prison—
Bars cannot conceal!
~Emily Dickinson

The only thing that is mine from birth
to death is my own life. Easily stolen,
but until then life is my own. I can waste it,

neglect it, mistreat it, forget how to use it,
and still it is mine, forever clinging.

I am the rightful owner of this life,
I may choose to celebrate, to honor the temple
in which I reside, to pay minute attention

where once I gave nothing but the back of my hand.
I could be grateful for life, all life,
even my own.

Moved by the Train

I like to see it lap the Miles,
And lick the valleys up,
And stop to feed itself at tanks;
And then, prodigious, step
Around a pile of mountains . . .
~Emily Dickinson

Much of my life has been spent near
railway trains. Their solemn whistles
a sonic background to my own solitude,

my life running on a parallel track, always
moving forward, often alone with only
that chugging soundtrack pushing me
to carry on.

Once again, my solitary habitat is so near
the railroad tracks, that horrid hooting
stanza drowns out all other sound,
nearly every hour of the day and night.

No one wants to hear a complaint
of loneliness at such a volume.
One of us has to go.

Blessings

Seeing the faces of my daughter, her
son and daughter on I morning
for the twenty-first I in a row.

Opening the fewest gifts we've shared
in all that time, we each received everything
we asked for. That is a true blessing.

No re-gifting to be done, no space to be found
for gifts we feel guilty to have received but
do not want, when so many have nothing.

Spending time with my friend who was once my partner,
for the first time in seven years, now she's back
    from Laredo.
She has spent too many holidays alone.

She now sometimes finds being with people,
even people she loves, draining.
Sharing our simple gifts was a blessing.

Watching the bevy of birds flock to the feeder
when they and I were the only ones awake
was a blessing. Goldfinches gave me
the gift of a rare appearance.

Our Library

A precious, mouldering pleasure 'tis
To meet an antique book . . .
. . . Old volumes shake their vellum heads
And tantalize, just so
~Emily Dickinson

Our library was not a room with high ceilings,
heavy velvet curtains at the French doors,
horsehair divans filled with choking dust to sit upon,
whilst dust motes floated before our eyes and heavy tomes
lay in our laps.

No leather-bound volumes lined shelves, no Chippendale
    desks sat in corners
waiting for us to write our thoughts
on vellum with ink and quill.

Our bookcase was handed down from mother
to daughter to daughter and to daughter,
so much the worse for wear—made of cherry
and white pine, mended with whatever was to hand,

not from care but from necessity, filled with books
collected from friends, relatives, and the town dump.
Favorites were read until the pages fell out

Several of the books from my own childhood
are now in my one and only bookcase.
    A. A. Milne's words are as much a part of me
as my own veins and blood.

The etiquette of Emily Post shaped and informed my life.
Radclyffe Hall's book, *The Well of Loneliness*, filled me
with compassion for the women I later came to love,
and the woman I became.

A Little Austere

You may think my lifestyle is a
little austere. The lack of abundance,
so few items, rather than multiples.

See the art on my walls? My carefully
selected books, my comfortable couch,
my one perfect chair? I sleep in the loft,

who needs more? This is not austerity,
this is simplicity, it is luxurious to have
everything I need and the freedom to say no,
no more, thank you.

Why Did You Invite Her?

Everyone hates to be a wet blanket,
yet soggy ground cloths save lives.

Find yourself in a kitchen with your stove
In flames and you'll wish you had
A blanket soaked in water or fire
retardant.

That's when you'll reach for your damp-palmed
friends, your party-poopers, your wallflowers,
those dour-faced loners who stand by,

waiting only for an opportunity to be of use,
are otherwise a damper on your ever-lasting fun.
Don't mind us, we'll be over here in the corner,
dripping.

Self-Made (a sijo*)

Having achieved success by my own efforts,
I am a self-made woman.

My education came from books,
and my life's experiences.

I wrote books, plays, and poems,
satisfaction rather than financial gain.

~~~

*A Sijo is an unrhymed Korean verse form that is usually 3 lines in length, averaging 14-16 syllables per line (for a poem total of 44-46 syllables).
- Line 1 introduces the situation or theme of the poem.
- Line 2 develops the theme with more detail or a "turn" in argument.
- Line 3 presents a "twist" and conclusion.

Gratitude

I deem that I with but a crumb
Am sovereign of them all.
~Emily Dickinson

I was born into poverty, but didn't notice
until I was grown and into a new reality.

In the US, because our starving children
are not photographed with flies in their eyes,
naked bellies protruding over mothers'
emaciated forearms, poverty can be unseen.

We were poor, but clean, my mother said.
We always had food of one kind or another.
We did not accept charity. We were privileged

not to endure racism. We were not recent immigrants.
We preferred to believe we were descended
from Native Americans. Instead, our ancestors
    participated in their genocide.

We were rich in troubles and secrets,
but also in values that allowed us to love our fellows,
never to steal, always to work, ever to share

what little we had. We were lucky to be filled
with love for others, instead of hate or resentment.
I don't know whether we choose our parents

before we're born. I don't know if reincarnation
is real. But gratitude is, and can make my life easier.
Therefore, I appreciate the life that made me

Battle scarred maybe, but I also wear the medals
of courage, resourcefulness, imagination,
and gratitude.

Act Five: Later Life

My age is as a lusty winter, frosty but kindly.

As You Like It
Act II, Scene 3

Artifacts

This is my baby book. A hand-me-down
from my dead brother, whose date of birth
is scratched out and my own written in.

This is the quilt I came home in
from the hospital. Note it is blue like the baby
book. Made for my brother, who died.

This is the pebble I swallowed when a baby.
Mom found it, cleaned it, kept it in a ring box
the rest of her life, as proof I survived.

This is my first stuffed toy, a rabbit in overalls
named Peanut because I couldn't say Peter,
and I wanted a girl. Stiff as the washboard
my mom cleaned her on. Now faded to gray
like my hair, she sits on my bed.

This is a picture of the headstone of my parents' grave.
He died in 1951. She saved money by having her name
and birth date engraved at the time. She died in 2012.
Was cremated.

This is forgiveness for Dad who died too young,
for Mom who didn't know how to mother,
and for myself for waiting so long to forgive.

Broke Broker Broken

I studied to be a broker, but firms
didn't want women back then,
or if they did, they had a quota
—already filled.

Now I'm just broke. Cash flow poor,
with no financial assets. Investments
used up, real estate all gone, and I'm
selling my car today.

You might think the economy
has broken me, but I refuse to fall
victim to that kind of talk. I have
a home, family, friends, and most
of my health.

My assets are the ability to imagine,
an open heart, a curious and open mind,
and a willing ear to lend anyone who
needs it.

I'm rich where it counts.
In here.

Still Here, Rain

Today I purchased *Dear Galileo* tickets
for a matinee performance on the playwright's birthday.
She promises to be in attendance and we'll all party
after with a champagne toast and a cake. She'll be thirty-
four-years old that day, and I was thirty-four once.

When I watered the plants on my balcony this morning,
I leaned over the edge and looked at the treetops.
They look dusty. We haven't had rain in weeks.
Day after day the temperature rises to ninety degrees
or more,

the humidity seems to fall in inverse proportion. Neither
the trees nor I bargained for such weather
in the Pacific Northwest. Not for weeks on end.
I can move away.

I was thirty-four once. And I am still here.
The trees are still here. It will rain again.
Maybe this week.

Scottish Ancestors

Next year will surely be the year I return to the
home of my ancestors. The land of thistle
and single-malt.

I will perform a small ceremony, throw a little
extra something on the fire, light a match,
and dance in the firelight, spin, twist, lift my limbs
until I am spent.

I will celebrate the old McCorkle woman
who held off the invaders of Argyllshire.
Because she lived while her entire family perished
at the hands of their enemy. She was allowed
to continue her life.

Alone with her memories, she tended a garden
of weeds she knew as herbs. Not for her
the Stockholm Syndrome. She gave her enemies tea,
and watched as one by one
they fell dead from an unknown illness.

Enough is Enough

When I am old, I shall wear purple,
she said. I refused to wait for the future,
and wore purple every day for ten years.
I swore I'd wear purple until "everyone"
came out. I meant Lily Tomlin, k.d. lang, Ellen.
They came out.

Now I am old, and wear purple,
turquoise, black, white, anything I like.
Whatever I choose to put on my body,
I wear with a sense of abandon.

Today I gave up being overweight.
No miracle diet. It was a change
of the mind. Overweight is a biased concept.
Bodies are what they are. I've given up
body-shaming, including my own.

Today, I am me. I own this body. This head.
This being that moves through the world.
I am strong, I am beautiful, I am enough.
I own my own temple. And I am queen
of all I survey in the mirror.

The Morning

Will there really be a "Morning?"
Is there such a thing as "Day?"
~Emily Dickinson

Time is but a construct,
a method for us to give order
To our lives.

Try telling me that lie
at 3 am when insomnia
has me by the throat.

If I could fly above
the matrix, would I see
where morning lies?

Would I learn how to stay
asleep in the dark, waiting
for the sun?

Who can tell me the truth? Who
will spread the answers at my feet,
like a lover?

Afterwards, Day

Our share of night to bear,
Our share of morning,
Our blank in bliss to fill,
Our blank in scorning . . .
Afterwards—Day!
~Emily Dickinson

Throwing off the covers, pulling
them on again. Lying on my side,
not sleeping. Turning to my back,
opening my eyes. Closing my
lids, meditating on relaxation of
every muscle. Hours tick slowly by.

Pain, when it comes in the night,
is fierce, unrelenting. Stronger than I am.
It takes hold, refusing to soften its grip,
shaking my soul as if to snap its neck.

Pain is the amnesiac that makes me forget
what my heart knows: it is always darkest
before dawn.

Sight

Before I got my eye put out,
I liked as well to see
As other creatures, that have eyes . . .,
~Emily Dickinson

A question often posed in our household
was which would you rather lose?
Hearing or eyesight.

As though we were doomed
to lose one or the other, if not
both.

Most chose hearing, as we are a family
of readers. Never mind the skies,
the city lights, the moon's aspects.

Never mind that losing our hearing means
never being able to recognize birds
by their calls, when we can't see
their winged visages.

At seventy, my ears are failing me,
my sense of smell has all but disappeared,
taste no longer enthuses over spices, but my
eyesight is improving. As is my appreciation
for all that I see.

Putting On

Every morning after I comb my hair
I put on my hearing aids, my partial plate,
and my glasses. My head is ready to go.

I don my clothes for the day, a shirt
some pants, my sandals. Or maybe a dress
if it's not yoga day. Now I'm ready
To play, or work, whichever I choose.

Maybe I'll run errands, or help a friend
with her chores. No one cares. To say
otherwise would be putting on airs.

Fun With Aging

Every time I open my mouth to say *How
to Get Away with Murder,* Jessica freaking
Fletcher takes over my vocal cords and I say
Murder She Wrote.

Stop it dammit, I am not that old.
I don't watch reruns of television shows
from my prime. I don't save bits of twine,
I don't try to shake out the last bit of anything.

Yes, I get the AARP magazine, but they send
that to everyone who turns fifty,
and fifty is the new thirty,
so that makes me only fifty now.

Oh, who am I kidding? I gave up looking
for a knight in shining armor thirty years ago,
when there was a chase-the-bad-guys show
on TV with a talking car, called *Knight Rider*.

I wonder when that's on . . .

Raves Are for the Young

Dylan Thomas wrote *Do not go gentle*
into that good night, Old age should burn
and rave at close of day;
Rage, rage against the dying of the light.

But I say instead: do your raging while you're young
or youngish anyway. As life runs out, your rage can, too,
it's time to overflow with love, share
what you have learned along the way.

Give your knowledge as freely as you pass along
your possessions, hand over the keys to your car.
Let someone else drive you around, give
your tired eyes a rest.

As the light dims, light a candle, put on music
that brings pleasure. Hold hands with the ones you love.
Go gently, go easily, go in peace.

Where There's Smoke

When faced with evidence of her ever-growing
forgetfulness, she wonders what other experiences
she has lost. She thinks she needs to remember
to tell her doctor of these incidents. A few minutes
later she wonders what the incidents were.
One was a movie. Now what was the other?

It doesn't matter, does it? Articles say there can be
causes she can do nothing about. She weaned
herself off the meds she could. She continues
to mete out the others into her pill calendar
to remember to take them. Except when she forgets.

Doctor says it's not Alzheimer's. Might be some
other form of dementia. Maybe she is having small
strokes. With so many migraines, how could she
tell the difference? It feels to her as if she recalls
the important things.

She hasn't forgotten the names of her children
yet. She remembers to keep to her routine
of writing every day. She never cooks, so no need
to wonder whether she left the stove on.
Her world is burning down without a fire.

All That Remains

All that remains after seven
decades is a human body,
a shambles, not its former self.

Wrinkled skin, sagging parts, battered joints,
clogged arteries, a broken and much repaired
heart still bursting its seams with love.

A human who sought love and freedom from
battery and pain. A woman who loved and lost
and gave her love to the wrong people

until she didn't. A mother who abandoned her first-born
to save them both. Who failed and succeeded and
tried again.

A grandmother who cherished her chance to do better,
be better, to love again.

All that remains is to live the next decades
with gratitude and grace.

Sunrise

"The east insisting on tomorrow."
~Traci Brimhall, "Nocturne with Oil Rigs and Jasmine"

As the end grows near I would hold
back tomorrow and live in yesterday

Or even the moment if I were strong like
some. But the Earth continues to spin

the east brings the sun and though
I hear time and space are but constructs

the sun rises and brings me
one day closer to eternal night.

AUTHOR'S AFTERWORD

When you read this collection, you may think I believe I have one foot in the grave. No. My mother lived to her mid-90s, and I see no reason why I won't live that long, or maybe longer. I write every day; there will be more books.

ACKNOWLEDGMENTS

I belong to three writing groups: Portland Lesbian Writers; East County San Diego Writers' Ink; and the Poem-A-Day group. Each of these groups has provided support and encouragement. The poem-a-day group does so daily. Without the expertise of the other poets, the support and encouragement from all these people, my poetry writing would be less frequent, and not as good. No one has supported my poetry more than my publisher. I am grateful every day for Lori L. Lake.

Portrait of the Poet as a Young Child

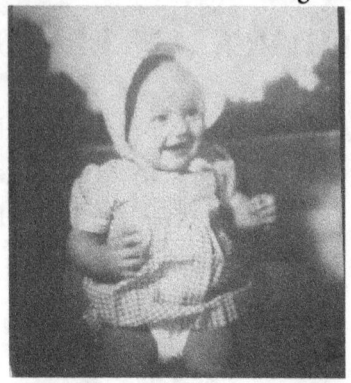

ABOUT THE POET

Sandra de Helen published her first poem at the age of fourteen. Her English teacher, Janice Wallace, submitted the poem to a teacher's magazine and surprised Sandra with a copy in print. The poem was about abortion, which was illegal at the time.

In her twenties, Sandra published a few poems in newspapers, which spurred her to take a Creative Writing Class at the local community college. The [male] professor professed she would never make a good poet because she didn't "write like a man." The next year she joined the women's movement and turned to writing plays.

Forty years later, she picked up Sage Cohen's book, *Writing the Life Poetic: An Invitation to Read and Write Poetry*, and resumed writing poems like a woman.

A long-time resident of Portland, Oregon, Sandra lives with her daughter and a very special cat.

Praise for Other Works by Sandra de Helen

Poetry

"[The poems in *All This Remains to be Discovered*] are a vulnerable, raw look at one's life with an undertone of tenderness and adult compassion and forgiveness. A very moving and worthwhile read."
~BuzzOregon

"These are fresh poems [in *Desire Returns for a Visit*] in every sense of the word. Flirty, audacious, original. A fresh take on Dickinson's love of women and words. A brazen exploration of the life cycle of love affairs. This book is an open-mouthed kiss to the reader. It will leave you breathless."
~G.L. Morrison, poet, lover of words, and short fiction writer

"I didn't need to read beyond the first line of the first poem to know I'd be loving this book."
~Lee Lynch, award-winning author of *Sweet Creek*

Plays

"[The stageplay] *The Clue in the Old Birdbath* is proving to be catnip for the robust, unadorned, unescorted females in attendance. Unfolding is a musical demolition by Sandra de Helen and Kate Kasten of Carolyn Keene's nubile teen detective Nancy Drew, here renamed Tansy True. Here, adolescent literature's beacon of girlish pluck and ingenuity is rendered into a salty, torpedo-breasted assassin of male domination."
~**Keith A. Joseph, Cleveland Scene**

Novels

"*The Hounding* is . . . an interesting and well-developed mystery. I recommend it for any Holmes/Watson obsessives."
~**Megan Casey, Lesbrary.com**

"I wish I had half the plotting talent that Sandra de Helen has. [*Till Darkness Comes*] is such a terrific and totally satisfying book."
~**Chelsea Cain, Thriller Writer, Humorist, and News Columnist**

"If you are a lover of Sherlock Holmes, [*The Illustrious Client*] is a fun look at what might happen had the characters been women and in the present day. The books' titles are taken from Sherlock Holmes' own stories and this book is loosely based on the one of the same title. However, this is not just a retelling of the Holmes stories. Ms. de Helen definitely makes it her own. The clues and red herrings as the pair solve the mystery are well placed. The plot was strong and interesting, and like a really good mystery, I couldn't figure out 'whodunnit' and was surprised by the reveal at the end."
~Long and Short Reviews.com

"[*The Hounding* is a] confident, meticulously detailed mystery that would have made Shirley [Comb's] pipe-smoking idol proud."
~Kirkus Reviews

"[*The Illustrious Client*] is certainly worth a read. With the author continuing to hone her talents, I am looking forward to the next one."
~Megan Casey, Lesbrary.com

www.ingramcontent.com/pod-product-compliance
Lightning Source LLC
Chambersburg PA
CBHW070114080526
44586CB00013B/1287